Eva O'Connor

Overshadowed

Bloomsbury Methuen Drama
An imprint of Bloomsbury Publishing Plc

B L O O M S B U R Y
LONDON • OXFORD • NEW YORK • NEW DELHI • SYDNEY

Bloomsbury Methuen Drama

An imprint of Bloomsbury Publishing Plc

Imprint previously known as Methuen Drama

50 Bedford Square	1385 Broadway
London	New York
WC1B 3DP	NY 10018
UK	USA

www.bloomsbury.com

Bloomsbury is a registered trade mark of Bloomsbury Publishing Plc

First published 2016

© Eva O'Connor, 2016

British Library Cataloguing-in-Publication Data
A catalogue record for this book is available from the British Library.

ISBN: PB: 978-1-4742-9108-8
ePub: 978-1-4742-9109-5
ePDF: 978-1-4742-9107-1

Library of Congress Cataloging-in-Publication Data
A catalog record for this book is available from the Library of Congress.

Typeset by Mark Heslington Ltd, Scarborough, North Yorkshire

Overshadowed

SUNDAY'S CHILD

Sunday's Child is an Irish theatre company founded in 2010, run by Eva O'Connor and Hildegard Ryan. They aim to create new, vibrant work that deals with issues that are often swept under the carpet. The company performs its work across Ireland and the UK, and has won various awards including the NSDF Best Emerging Artist Award (Edinburgh Fringe, 2012), the First Fortnight Award (Dublin Fringe, 2014), the Argus Angel Award (Brighton Fringe, 2015) and the Fishamble Award for Best New Writing (Dublin Fringe, 2015).

Eva O'Connor is a writer and performer from Ogonnelloe, Co. Clare, Ireland. She has been writing, performing and producing her own work with Sunday's Child since 2010. She has a degree in English Literature and German from the University of Edinburgh, and an MA in Theatre Ensemble from Rose Bruford College of Theatre and Performance, London.

Hildegard Ryan is a director and script editor from Skerries, Co. Dublin. She has a first-class degree in English Literature and History from Trinity College, and a filmmaking diploma from Central Film School, London.

Eva and Hildegard live in London.

ORIGINAL CAST

IMOGENE	**Roseanne Lynch**
CAOL	**Eva O'Connor**
FIONNUALA	**Sinéad Clancy**
TARA	**Maeve O'Sullivan**
EAMONN	**Adam Devereux**

Overshadowed was first performed at the Tiger Dublin Fringe, where it won the Fishamble Award for Best New Writing 2015. It was then performed at Skerries Soundwaves Festival 2015. *Overshadowed* runs at Project Arts Centre, Dublin, as part of the First Fortnight Festival 2016 and then goes on to Theatre503 in London.

Written by Eva O'Connor
Directed by Hildegard Ryan
Dramaturgy by Hildegard Ryan
Set and costume design by Deirdre Dwyer
Lighting design by Tara Doolan
Music by Daniel Cummins

Overshadowed

Characters

Imogene, *17. Suffering from anorexia. Once vibrant and outgoing she has recently become thin and withdrawn.*

Caol, *the personification of anorexia. A manipulative, possessive creature determined to control all aspects of Imogene's life.*

Tara, *16. Imogene's younger sister. An irrepressible extravert, who adores her older sister.*

Fionnuala, *46. The girls' mother. A strong, capable loving woman, recently divorced.*

Eamonn, *18. Imogene's crush. Charismatic, manic, misunderstood.*

Imogene's Letter to Eamonn I

Imogene Dear Eamonn,

I am writing this from ICU. The place is completely silent apart from the beeping monitors and humming machines. Everyone is tense; families shuffle in and out willing loved ones to pull through, staff work around the clock. It's all very surreal. But despite all that, I'm thinking surprisingly clearly. Maybe it's cos I'm sitting still. It's so long since I sat in one place. I didn't realise how frantic I was living until now. Hanging out with you was one of the few things that made me feel calm, slowed the pace of my frantic heart. I wanted to tell you that, and other things that I don't think I expressed very well. I know you don't like reading, but I'm hoping you'll make an exception for this letter.

I used to be hilarious. I used to tell terrible rambling jokes, which went on for up to eleven minutes and weren't funny at all, but people always laughed. Hysterically. I used to be wild. I used to drink litre bottles of blue WKD and piss in the queue for Sapphire's.

I used to do things on whims. I once set up a car boot sale with all my mother's furniture when she was at work cos she was being stingy with pocket money. I used to leg it through the fields because I loved the feel of the scratchy grass against my bare legs, not because I was desperate to burn calories. And Eamonn, by far the most impressive thing about the old me was that I was absolutely class at the worm.

Scene One

Imogene (*age 13*) *and* **Tara** (*age 12*) *are lying belly down on the kitchen floor laughing.* **Fionnuala** *is sitting at the kitchen table sipping wine, observing her daughters fondly.*

Fionnuala Girls I'm serious that floor is not clean.

Imogene It is Mum look!

Imogene *licks the floor.*

Fionnuala   Imogene Walsh you animal, don't lick my kitchen floor with your filthy tongue, that's vile!

Tara *laughs, licks the floor, then winces.*

Imogene   You're always saying it's clean enough to eat our dinner off!

Fionnuala   Christ alive! You'd think it was in a zoo you were raised!

Imogene *licks the floor again and starts to worm across the kitchen floor.* **Tara** *screeches with delight.*

Fionnuala   My god you look like some kind of deranged worm.

Tara   Imo teach me please! I can't do it. Stop stop stop! I want to learn!

Imogene   OK, so you use your arms to push yourself off the ground like this. Work those biceps. And then you just go for it. It's all about commitment.

Tara   I can't!

Imogene   Of course you can. You just have to believe. Visualise yourself doing it. See the worm and then be the worm.

Fionnuala   You sound like some kind of mad spiritual leader.

Tara   Be quiet Mum I'm trying to concentrate!

Imogene   It helps if you chant. I'm a worm I'm a worm I'm a mighty fine worm!

Tara   I'm a worm, I'm a worm, I'm a mighty useless worm!

Fionnuala   Girls why don't you ever do *ballet* in the kitchen? The O'Dwyer girls down the road are prodigies at the ballet apparently. Lucy the youngest one just got a place in one of those prestigious ballet places in London would you believe. Hardly surprising I suppose. They have the figures for it. So tall and elegant. They're like thoroughbred race horses.

Tara   Race horses don't do ballet.

Imogene   Ya Mum would you ever shut up about the O'Dwyer girls and come down here and worm with us?

Tara   *Ya Mum*, you're always going on about joining an exercise class. This will make you sweat!

Fionnuala   You must be joking me.

Imogene   It's a brilliant toning exercise, tums bums and biceps!

Tara   It's a full body worm out!

Fionnuala *reluctantly decides to attempt the warm, and joins the girls on the floor.*

Fionnuala   Yer mad as hatters! If your father walks in now he'll have us all committed! Sure you're as loopy as his patients.

The girls giggle.

Fionnuala   Well are you gonna show me or not?!

Tara   I'm gonna get it this time, I can feel it!

Imogene   Put your hands further back. No like this. OK, all together now I'm a worm I'm a worm I'm a mighty fine worm!

Tara *and* **Imogene** *take off, worming across the floor.* **Fionnuala** *collapses on her stomach, laughing.*

Imogene's Letter to Eamonn II

Imogene   When I was fourteen Dad left. Sometimes in the middle of the night we'd wake up to the sound of them screeching at each other. Tara used to block her ears, scrunch up her face and sing *Spice Up Your Life* to herself. I used to slag her for it, but in fairness to her I think it worked, she claims she can't remember any of it.

I suppose it was all pretty run of the mill, as failed marriages go, Dad was rarely around, and then eventually he wasn't at all. But it's a shitty thing to happen, to lose a parent like that. I don't know why I'm telling you this, I know you've been through so much worse. I suppose I'm just acknowledging the past. Because all those shit things that happen to us, they all affect us somehow. They make us who we are.

Scene Two

Imogene (*now 17*) *is looking in the mirror, sucking in her stomach, adjusting her school skirt.* **Tara** (*now 16*) *is lying on the floor painting her nails orange. She is wearing pink silk pyjamas.* **Caol** *is lurking in the background.*

Tara   I'm so bad at this! Imo can you do my left hand? I spilt the whole bottle of remover on the sitting room carpet so if I mess up I'll have orange fingers forever!

Caol *slowly begins to approach* **Imogene** *from behind.*

Tara   Imogene I *need* you!

Imogene   Why are you painting your nails before school? You'll get detention.

Tara   No I won't. I'll pick it off on the bus. I'll do yours after if you want. To match your outfit.

Imogene   No thanks.

Tara   I have loads of different colours. I have at least fifty shades. But don't worry none of them are grey.

Hello! Your bum looks great in that.

Imogene   Eh no it doesn't. It's a school skirt. Now can you please leave I'm trying to get ready.

Tara   Stop compliment fishing. You're an absolute babe station no matter what you wear. Jenny O'Sullivan wears her skirt like that.

Imogene   Does she?

Tara   Ya, but you're hotter.

Imogene *suddenly realises that* **Tara** *has been painting her nails on her maths notes.*

Imogene   Tara, they're my maths notes! I need those!

Tara   Chill the beans, it's only a few sums.

Imogene   They're covered in nail varnish! I have a test today and now I'm gonna fail!

Tara   Think of it as orange highlighter.

Imogene   Just get out of my room. I can't think straight with you in here. You're not even dressed.

Tara   Ya I am, I'm wearing these.

Imogene   Get out!

Tara *flounces out of the room.* **Imogene** *continues to study herself in the mirror. She senses* **Caol** *at her feet for the first time.*

Imogene   Who are you?

Caol   Caol is me Caol is my name // Caol is the name of the hunger games.

Imogene   Why are you, why are you in my room?

Caol   I am no stranger, we've flirted before // but now you need me to keep the score // to tip the balance, to balance the scales // I've watched you panic, flounder and flail // I'll guard and guide, I'll conquer control // I'll be the companion of your suffering soul.

Imogene   Wait what? No! No, this is not what I . . . I don't need you. There are things about myself I need to – want to change, but I can do it on my own. I never asked for –

Caol   True friends don't wait to be called // look at you, so helpless and flawed // I can help you conquer your weight // diminish the load, lessen your freight // you're seething at the seams with discontent // every ounce of energy spent // on loathing your body grabbing at flesh // I'll change you completely put me to the test.

Imogene   I don't even know you.

Caol   Lies girl, sweet little lies // you know who I am, look at those eyes // that desperate longing to shrivel and fade // I'll be your ally your starvation aide.

Imogene   You're right I do know who you are. I've seen you at school with other girls. But I think you've confused me with someone else . . . I'm not –

Caol   You want a taste of my delicious control // you want me to enter your floundering soul // the rules? Restraint refusal retreat // I'll teach you to conquer the will to eat.

Imogene   I, I appreciate the offer really, but –

Caol   I don't mean to intrude, don't mean to pry // but your life is in chaos this room is a sty // and you're failing maths did I overhear? // You're spiralling out of control I fear //

Imogene   Stop please! I know all this, you don't need to remind me!

Caol   I only come to those who silently plead // If you don't want me here then just ask me to leave.

Imogene   Wait! Don't go . . . yet. I'm sorry I'm just a bit flustered. What exactly would all this entail?

Caol   I can help you look like Jenny O'Dwyer // a long, lean, elegant wire // let's give little Jenny a run for her money // the taste of victory will be as sweet as honey.

Imogene   What do you mean victory?

Caol   Can't you see I can help you swim not sink? // I can help you stop eating and start to *think* // with clarity, conviction, concise control // no more messy room, no unfulfilled goals.

Imogene   I admit that does sound kind of appealing. But what will other people think?

Caol   I'll lurk in the shadows, no one will know // my powers of thinness to you I'll bestow.

Imogene   I'd like that. It just feels like quite a big decision . . .

Caol   You're not on the fence you've had all your life // to woo me here you've made your choice // say yes to me it's the sweetest deal // I'll change everything, how you look and feel.

Imogene *gazes into* **Caol**'s *eyes.*

Imogene   Yes.

Scene Three

Imogene *is skipping in her room.* **Caol** *is tapping the floor rhythmically, urging her on.* **Tara** *enters.*

Imogene   I'm busy.

Tara   Busy skipping? What are you a professional boxer now? It's my birthday.

Imogene (*breathless*)   I know. Happy birthday.

Caol   Happy birthday to you, happy birthday to you happy birthday dear disgusting comfort eating little sister, interfering ugly twister. Happy birthday to you.

Tara   We are leaving in five minutes. Come in your sweaty skipping gear, I honestly don't mind. It won't be the same without you.

Caol   You're not going so don't waste your breath // ignore her look at me instead.

Imogene   Just get drunk and you won't notice I'm not there.

Tara   Come on Imo! Please I need someone to help me babysit Mum. You know what she's like when she gets a few glasses of wine into her.

Caol   Her attempts to lure you are almost comical // now banish this child, let's be economical // with our precious time we've none to lose // now opt out decline simply refuse.

Tara   I'm sorry we're going to a stupid restaurant. I should have thought of that before. I know eating out isn't really your thing . . . I'd cancel, but all the girls are meeting us there. I looked up the menu online, and they have nice grilled fish, and salads, or you could just have G and Ts for main course?

Imogene   Just go Tara. Have a great night. Go crazy. And I'll see you when you're home. I might still be awake.

Tara   Can I have a hug?

Imogene   I'm really sweaty, and you're all dressed up.

Tara   OK. Fine. See you later.

Tara *leaves, looking crestfallen. Once she is gone,* **Imogene** *stops skipping, and collapses with her head in her hands, plagued with guilt.*

Caol   Meddling sister interfering // can't bear to see you disappearing // green-eyed monsters in her veins // wishes she had the strength to change // Finally she's gone the silence is gold // let's use it wisely before the night grows old // I'm brimming with pride you're gaining ground // now get back to skipping and shedding those pounds.

Scene Four

Tara *enters* **Imogene**'s *room at 3 in the morning, drunk. She kicks off her high heels, and flops down on* **Imogene**'s *bed.* **Imogene** *wakes, but* **Caol**'s *who is curled up in the corner, remains asleep.*

Tara   I came home.

Imogene (*sleepy*)   Hey.

Tara   I was gonna go back with some Brazilian lad, but I decided to come home to you instead.

Imogene   Aw thanks T dog.

Tara *barks*.

Tara   I wouldn't have, apart from he ran away. A Brazilian ran away from me on my birthday. Can you believe that? We were on the bus home, and two stops into the journey he just spontaneously hopped off. Practically threw himself out of a moving bus to get away from me. Jesus! And he refused to sing me Happy Birthday in Spanish.

Imogene   I believe they speak Portuguese in Brazil.

Tara   Now you tell me.

Imogene   So how was it?

Tara   The hot Brazilian sex that never happened?

Imogene   Your birthday night out. I was thinking of you.

Tara   Pretty good. I think. It's all a bit of a blur.

Imogene   Sign of a good night.

Tara   Me and the girls went clubbing in Sapphire's. Demented Delaney was there. That I remember all too clearly. Cheek of him crashing my birthday. He makes my skin crawl.

Imogene   He's always in Sapphire's is he not. He was hardly there especially for your birthday.

Tara   He definitely was. He's such a fucking creep. No he's not even a creep, creeps I can deal with. He's a complete and utter nut-job. He stripped naked on the dance floor and was helicoptering his dick around the place at the same time as trying to sell us rip-off, dodgy pills.

Imogene   Sounds kind of entertaining.

Tara   It was vile, that's what it was. He touched me on my bare leg with his drug dealer penis!

Imogene *laughs.*

Imogene   Was the food nice?

Tara   What?

Imogene   The food in the Chinese, was it nice?

Tara   It was OK.

Imogene   What did you have?

Tara   I don't remember. Why do you care what I ate? You could have at least come dancing after the meal, protected me from Demented Delaney.

Imogene   I'm sorry Tara, I just didn't have the energy.

Tara   You were skipping like Katie Taylor when I left. Did you finally wear yourself out?

Caol *wakes up.*

Caol   What's she doing here in the dead of night? // we need our rest get her out of my sight.

Imogene   I don't want to fight with you Tara. You should go to bed. You must be exhausted.

Tara   Can I sleep here tonight?

Imogene *and* **Caol**   No.

Tara   I knew you'd say that. You used to be a yes person.

Imogene   What's that supposed to mean?

Tara   I'm serious. You used to be up for everything. You used to be the life and soul of the party. You used to be the one going home with Spaniards. Tonight in the club I did the worm across the dance floor. And the whole club cheered.

Imogene   I'm sure you were tearing up the dance floor.
Literally. Here, T, I'm sorry but I need to sleep now I'm
wrecked. Please . . .

Caol *and* **Imogene**   Leave!

Tara   You're not listening to me! Tonight in the club I did
the worm across the dance floor. And the crowd were loving
it. But as they all whooped and cheered, all I could think of
was you and how we always used to do it together, in the
kitchen, on the beach, at bus stops. Remember that time we
were doing it outside Ryan's bar and I cut my chin on some
glass and you thought I had slit my throat? But tonight I just
couldn't keep going. I just stopped mid-worm and lay face
down on the dance floor and the security guy rushed over to
see if I had K.O.'d. I just felt so sad you weren't there. So sad
I was paralysed.

Imogene   So sad you were *paralysed*? For christ sake Tara,
you're seventeen. It's about time you got your own life. I'm
sick of you constantly invading my space, and trying to guilt
trip me just cos I don't want to spend every minute of the
day with you. It's pathetic. You're a leech. You know that?
Get out!

Tara   You're not the same person who taught me how
to worm.

Tara *storms out of the room.* **Caol** *wraps herself around* **Imogene**
possessively.

Scene Five

Imogene *is smoking behind a dilapidated prefab at school.* **Caol** *is
perched on a height above* **Imogene**, *stroking her hair.* **Eamonn**
appears, shadow boxing, punching the air violently. He sees
Imogene, *but pretends not to and almost punches her in the face.*

Imogene   Jesus.

Caol *wraps herself possessively around* **Imogene**'s *shoulders ready to step in and defend her at any moment.*

Eamonn   Mary and Joseph. Sorry, did I scare ya, ya sensitive soul? Did I put the wind up ya?

Caol   The sight of him would scare anyone // filthy dirty cheeky scum.

Eamonn   Shouldn't you be in class?

Imogene   Shouldn't you?

Eamonn   Touché.

Eamonn *casually starts doing press-ups, with claps in between.*

Eamonn   So what class you skivin so, ya big rebel ya?

Imogene   I'm not skiving. I wasn't feeling well. I'm just getting some air.

Eamonn   Is it women's problems you're having? Is it that bloody time of month again? I won't ask any more so. Ignorance is bliss as they say.

Imogene   I fainted in class.

Eamonn   From the heavy blood loss was it?

Caol   We choose to refrain from periods // refuse to bleed as they demand we should // Don't tell us we need a healthy womb // fertile life is doom and gloom // excess blood is a sign of weakness // we don't subscribe to all this leakiness.

Imogene   I get light-headed sometimes. I have health issues.

Caol   It's them in there with the health issues // with the rolls of teenage fat tissue // increasing numbers on the scales // it's them with problems, them that have failed.

Eamonn   They say you should sit with your head between your legs if you feel faint. I can sit with my head between your legs if you don't feel up to doing it yourself.

Imogene   You're offering to go down on me on my period?

Caol   Creepy crawly pervy boy // I know his game his sleazy ploy //

Eamonn   Well you don't have your period clearly. Look at you there's barely enough meat on ya to keep you alive never mind a baby.

Imogene   My sister warned me about you. She said you're so mental you're not even fit to be in school.

Eamonn   Ah Jesus would you calm down princess. I was only stating the obvious. No need to get all psycho bitchy on me.

Imogene   You're the psycho.

Eamonn (*mocking*)   No you're the psycho. No *you're* the psycho . . . Maybe we're both psychos.

Caol   Don't let him tar you with his crazy brush // now end this nonsense I've had enough //

Eamonn   Can I tap a fag off ya? Ah go on, I'm gaspin.

Imogene *reluctantly offers him a cigarette.*

Caol   Don't share with him don't interact // this boy is scum and that's a fact.

Eamonn   Camels eh? Expensive taste. Too good to roll your own are you, ya big princess ya?

Imogene   Ya, I'm far too middle-class for that kind of craic.

Eamonn   Normally I'm on my own out here. It's nice having company.

Imogene   That's what us gals are for. That's why god made Eve after all. Out of a tiny piece of Adam's rib. Couldn't even be bothered to make us from scratch, but sure I'm sure he had better things to be doing.

Eamonn   Do you know what I reckon? I reckon Eve came first. Shoved Adam out her vagina and as soon as he could speak he started spreading vicious rumours that Eve was just an afterthought, and that she force fed him some poisonous fruit and women are useless cunts, blah de fuckin blah. And ever since then men have been a shower of cruel ungrateful wankers, and somehow got away with it.

Imogene   Wow. That is a very interesting take on creation. Is that your chat-up line? You tell all the girls your ground-breaking theory about us being the superior species, then you unzip your fly, and depending on how good the service is you might give them a toke of a joint as a reward?

Eamonn   I don't know who your sources are but you got yourself some false information love. D'ya hear me . . . Anna baby?

Imogene   What did you call me?

Eamonn   Nothing. Eh, what's your name again?

Imogene   You called me Anna, I heard you.

Imogene *rushes over to* **Eamonn** *who is doing press-ups again, with a fag in his mouth, and kicks him over.*

Eamonn   Jesus, relax would you!

Caol   Anna they name us, with their jealous tongues // Anna girl they whisper the lighter we become // sticks and stones will break our bones, words will only make us thinner // make us vomit up our dinner.

Imogene   That's not my name.

Eamonn (*imitating the Ting Tings' song 'That's Not My Name'.*) They call me Mary, they call me Nora, they call me Anna That's not my name, that's not my name, d'ya remember that song?! That was fierce catchy back in the day. Who sang that was it the Cheeky Girls?

Imogene   Fuck you.

Imogene *grabs the cigarette from* **Eamonn***'s mouth and tosses it on the floor.*

Eamonn   Oi! I was smoking that!

Eamonn *picks the cigarette off the ground.*

Eamonn   I'm sorry *Imogene* for getting your name wrong. I do apologise for any offence caused. I'm Eamonn by the way. While we are on the subject of names. Like De Valera, Dunphy. All the greats.

Imogene   I know your name.

Eamonn   Course you do, wha?

Eamonn *winks.*

Imogene   Demented Delaney. A dealer of every narcotic under the sun.

Eamonn   Listen to me, *Imogene*. I'm many things; I'm a gymnast, I'm a philosopher, I'm a savage cook, I'm not just a dealer. Right?

Imogene   Right.

Eamonn   I'm glad we're on the same page. See ya round Imo baby.

Eamonn *winks at her and strolls off.*

Imogene's Letter to Eamonn III

Imogene   I can't remember exactly when things got really bad. I suppose that's the nature of a slippery slope, you can plummet pretty deep, pretty fast and not even notice.

Scene Six

Imogene *and* **Caol** *are in* **Imogene***'s bedroom.* **Caol** *begins to interrogate* **Imogene** *about an incident that occurred that day in school.*

Caol   What happened today? // What happened today that made you stray?

Imogene   I don't know. I'm sorry. Can we just not talk about it, for now. For five minutes. It was just a minor –

Caol   Disaster of the unmitigated variety // and now you're full of remorse full of anxiety?

Imogene   All day my head was, my mind was blurry, swaying, like I was looking through someone else's really strong glasses, I couldn't focus, I couldn't . . .

Caol   Straight-ly think? I saw that plain // she's lost it I thought, she's gone insane // Look at you, you biscuit savage // you deserve to be punished, to be ruined and ravaged.

Imogene   I panicked. And I know I should have politely refused it. I should have smiled and clenched my teeth until my jaw ached just in case someone dared to force feed me. Or I should have politely accepted it, crushed it in my fist, and scattered it crumb by crumb into a neat little Hansel and Gretel trail.

Caol   So now she's referencing nursery rhymes // making light of her disgusting crimes.

Imogene   Or or . . . having been stupid enough, weak enough to let it cross my lips I should have legged it to the bathroom, rammed my fingers down my throat and retched, until I regurgitated every last morsel, along with the entire acidic contents of my empty stomach. That's what I *should* have done. I know. Sure isn't hindsight a great thing?

Caol   How dare you address me with that sarcastic tone // you'll pay for this now we're alone.

Caol *begins to forcefully undress* **Imogene**, *ripping the buttons on her school shirt and poking at her flesh.*

Imogene (*pleading*)   It's Friday! It's the weekend. It's when people let their hair down. They straighten it, they curl it, they go to parties, they get drunk, they shift each other. They have *fun*. And on Monday they come in with stories and secrets and scandals. That used to be me. I used to have a life, I used to live for the weekend like everyone else. But I don't get that Friday feeling any more. Friday means nothing to me now. It doesn't mean freedom, or fun – it means more time to exercise, it means forty-eight hours of no school while we hole up in here, and control and calculate, monitor and minimise, and hit targets. Or in my case fail to. And today I just snapped.

Caol   Snapped? Are you some kind of elastic band // you did not snap, you exploded, expanded // outwards by miles I can see it clear // in your arms, your face, your thighs, your ears // in your all-over body, in your biscuit flesh // you're a failed anna girl, you're a pitiful mess // You're a pile of crumbly lippidy mush // there's nothing more to be discussed.

Imogene   I'm so tired. I've been working so hard. I earned a fucking custard cream.

Caol   So now she thinks she's entitled to a biscuit? // you think you can unravel, destroy, risk it // you're worse, you're weaker than I had ever foreseen // and now it's over you killed the dream // And now let's pay a visit to our friend the scales // at the thought of the figures my mind shivers and pales // you'll pay your weight in sorries mark my words // I've locked the door so we won't be disturbed.

Imogene (*struggling to breathe*)   No, not yet please, I can't breathe. I just want two minutes without my mind being hijacked . . . And yes, I want to shrink of course I do, but it's my body that I want to disappear, not my mind. My mind is shrivelling, it's collapsing in on itself and this is not what I . . . I can't breathe please, not the scales, not now please . . .

Caol   Sshhh my child forgiveness will come // I hate to see you come undone // but only the scales can erase this transgression // to rescue you from this food depression // Control is our weapon in this life this war // it's our reward what we're striving for // it's our saving grace it's what numbs the pain // the more pounds we shed the more power we gain //

Caol *drags* **Imogene** *along the ground, and forces her on to the scales.* **Imogene**, *who is now crying, refuses to look down.* **Caol** *gazes down at the flickering numbers, then slaps* **Imogene** *across the face. She falls to the ground.* **Tara** *bursts in and rushes over to help* **Imogene**.

Tara   Imo! What happened? Are you OK?

Imogene   Ya, I'm fine.

Tara   You don't look fine.

Imogene   Get off me Tara. What are you doing in here? Jesus I don't even have privacy in my own room.

Tara   I was just checking if you were OK . . . I heard a thump and I –

Imogene   Leave me the fuck alone!

Scene Seven

Tara *is standing in her school uniform at the front of her class, about to read an essay she has written.* **Tara**'s *hands are shaking. She has orange nail varnish on.*

Tara   Living in the shadow of my older sister. Oh god. I'm shaking. You all know I'm dyslexic as fuck so I probably won't even get to the end of this. Sorry, sorry, I'm dyslexic as *anything* . . .

For years, as us younger siblings tend to do, I idolised my older sister, I copied her, dressed like her, tagged along with her friends and considered her an authority on every subject under the sun, from which was the best Barbie (the vet Barbie of course because she was clever and saved animals, whilst still looking great), which Power Ranger was the best (the pink one of course because she was a Power Ranger and she wore pink) which role I should play in the sitting room shows we put on for our parents (she usually advised me to play the tortured servant, while she took on the more challenging, glamorous role of the cruel mistress). I never minded. It was enough just to grace the sitting-room stage with her.

Eventually she ousted me from her friendship circle and demanded that I stop following her everywhere (including and particularly into the loo). She even made me walk a few paces behind her on the way to school. We grew apart but I remained willingly in her shadow. That shadow was sometimes a cold and dark place. I worried about never being as clever, as popular, as magnetic as her.

If someone had told me years ago that one day my sister's personality would be less vibrant, her laugh would be less infectious, her eyes less sparkly, I would have dismissed it as nonsense, but perhaps a tiny part of me would have welcomed their strange prediction. Finally she would stop stealing the sisterly limelight.

But in the last year that's exactly what has happened and it has broken my heart. My vibrant, vivacious older sister is fading away. Or at least that's what so many people close to her fear, what people whisper behind her back in school. I know in my heart, however, that she is not an ounce less of the person I grew up with. She is not vanishing before our eyes, she is simply living in the shadow of a formidable illness. This shadow is long and all-consuming. It does not shift as the sun rises and sets, but remains around the clock draining her strength, eclipsing her.

That illness is anorexia nervosa, a condition so many people associate with fad diets, or the quest for the perfect bikini body. But anorexia is not a teenaged whim. It is a monster. It's a creature that infiltrates the mind and destroys the body. It is a toxic companion that accompanies the sufferer into darker territories than most of us will ever pass through.

Only Imogene can banish her demons, only Imogene can beat anorexia. But I intend to walk ten steps behind, just as we used to on the way to school. And one day, she will shake this shadow. One day her radiant big sister's light will shine so brightly that it will obliterate this illness, and the world will need sunglasses just to look at her.

Scene Eight

Tara *and* **Fionnuala** *are in the kitchen. They are about to have dinner. There is a salad on the table especially for* **Imogene**, *who has yet to come down from her room. The sound of* **Imogene** *and* **Caol** *skipping can be heard through the ceiling.*

Fionnuala   Where is your sister?

Tara   In her room by the sounds of it. Mum, I need 200 euro for the deposit for the school trip. It has to be in by Friday.

Fionnuala   I've called her three times now. If I can hear her, then surely she can hear me. That thumping. Jesus!

Tara   You said I could go, ages ago, as a present for not failing the junior cert. Remember? You promised you'd pay for it.

Fionnuala   You know I really thought the skipping was just a fad, that she'd get bored of it. I took the rope off her last week, fat lot of good that did.

Tara   I think she has a secret stash. Most teenagers hide drugs or condoms, Imogene hides skipping ropes. Eh Mother, can you write me that cheque please?

Fionnuala   You're not going.

Tara   What? It's not like we don't have the money. If you won't give it to me I'll ask Dad.

Fionnuala   Don't you *dare* ask him for anything. Do you hear me?

Tara   Why are you always such a dragon? You've just decided spontaneously to punish me?

Fionnuala   This isn't about you Tara. Look, if I let you go, I have to let *her* go.

Fionnuala *gestures to the ceiling, where the thumping is coming from.*

Fionnuala   And if *she* goes she'll come back in a coffin.

Tara   You're disgusting. Do you know that?! Why would you even say that. I've lost my appetite.

Fionnuala   Oh so now you're not eating either? Brilliant! Let's all have celery and green tea for dinner!

Tara   You're one to talk. You're always on some fad diet. Aren't you on the 5.2 right now?

Fionnuala   There is a difference between sensible eating and starving yourself! *Imogene*!

Tara   There's pine nuts in that.

Fionnuala   There *are* pine nuts in it. Yes. A few.

Tara   She won't eat it.

Fionnuala   Oh yes she will.

Tara   I'm just saying she won't touch it if there's pine nuts in it.

Caol *enters,* **Imogene** *trailing close behind.*

Caol   Well well well, if it isn't dinner time // sinner time, the desperate attempt to prevent us from getting thinner time // Ingest digest? Protest we will!

Fionnuala   Very generous of you to grace us with your presence Imogene.

Imogene   What's this?

Fionnuala   A salad.

Caol   A salad she says. And what's lying in wait under that bed of leaves // what fattening substance has she poorly concealed?

Imogene   There's pine nuts in this.

Tara   Told you.

Fionnuala   There *are* pine nuts in it, yes. A minuscule handful.

Caol *drapes herself over* **Imogene**'s *shoulders and the two of them stare into the bowl. She holds up a bottle of Weight Watchers dressing.*

Fionnuala   I bought you this today.

Only half a point per serving it says. Whatever that means. I have to admit I was a bit sceptical, but I tried it and it's delicious. I might even have some myself.

Imogene *and* **Caol**   No!

Imogene   Thank you.

Fionnuala   Honestly Imogene, there's nothing in it. A few chemicals I'm sure, but no calories at all. It will jazz up those sad lettuce leaves.

Imogene   I'm not hungry. I ate at school.

Fionnuala   I'm sure you did pet. But there's always room for a few lettuce leaves.

Imogene *and* **Caol** *are now intertwined and rocking back and forward in the chair.*

Imogene   I don't want any dressing.

Fionnuala   But I bought it especially for you. It was four euro for this little bottle Imogene.

Imogene   I said I don't want it.

Fionnuala   Just a tiny drizzle. There you go. Just a little drop on each leaf. It's delicious. Trust me. I'll leave it there in case you want any more.

Imogene *and* **Caol** *stare at the salad.*

Fionnuala   Imogene I do not want to fight you at the dinner table.

Imogene   I . . .

Imogene *and* **Caol**   Don't want it!

Fionnuala   Tara and I are not leaving the table until you've eaten what's in front of you.

Tara   This is fucked. You know she's not letting me go on the school tour because of you!

Imogene   What? What has the school tour got to do with anything?

Fionnuala   Eat your salad Imogene!

Caol *bangs on* **Imogene**'s *chair, and* **Imogene**, *obeying* **Caol**'s *instruction, shoves the bowl away from her.* **Fionnuala** *waits a moment, removes the bowl and smashes it on the floor.*

Fionnuala   Fine!

Scene Nine

Fionnuala *is alone in the kitchen. She is preparing to call her ex-husband to ask for help with* **Imogene**'s *illness.* **Imogene**'s *frantic skipping can be heard through the ceiling.*

Fionnuala   Hi John, it's me, Colette. Yes, hi. It has indeed. A few years I suppose. I've lost track. I'm not interrupting your evening I hope. Oh 'House of Cards', I see. I mean I have seen an episode or two, but I certainly don't watch it religiously, that Claire woman irritates me so much, completely puts me off it, to be honest. What fifty-year-old woman looks like that?

Yes we are all fine. Well actually . . . (*Deep breath.*) That's why I'm calling. We're not fine. It's Imogene John. She's not eating properly. Starving herself actually. Yes. A while now, six months, a year. I don't know. She's always been funny with food.

Of course I have, but she hardly speaks these days. And you can't force feed a teenager I'll tell you that much for nothing. She hides it well, I didn't realise how thin she was until I saw her in her swimsuit last week. I got the fright of my life. She's a skeleton. You can see her spine, her hip bones, she's literally skin and bone. I could hardly bear to look at her. And I have the school breathing down my neck, saying that other pupils are concerned about her condition. She's up all night exercising and I can hear skipping through the walls. She's like a ghost. A manic ghost. And I'm back on the Xanax John. I'm back on the Xanax.

No John, please don't. We don't need you here, that would just complicate things, trust me. Can't you arrange something from where you are? Talk to your psychiatrist mates, figure out the options. Nothing you can't do over the phone.

Yes, someone mentioned St Pat's . . . So I hear. Three months? No John, three months is . . . You don't understand. I just don't think she can wait that long. (*Pause. She is almost crying.*) I'm just so worried about her John. (*She composes herself.*) Let's not please, it's too late for all that. Just let me know. As soon as possible. Thank you, I appreciate it. Right well, I'll let you get back to 'House of Cards'. Bye John.

Fionnuala *hangs up the phone.* **Imogene**'s *skipping ceases abruptly as the collapses.*

Scene Ten

Eamonn *is sitting behind the prefabs. He has a cut on his hand and blood all over him. He is attempting to bandage it up with toilet roll.* **Imogene** *rounds the corner,* **Caol** *following unusually far behind her.*

Imogene   Hey.

Eamonn *attempts to hide his hand before* **Imogene** *can see it.*

Eamonn   Well Imo. Any craic?

Imogene   Hey.

Eamonn   Bloody glamorous wha?

Imogene   You in trouble?

Eamonn   Ah sure I'm always in trouble. Never a dull moment. Speakin of trouble, I saw you waiting outside Fitzy's office yesterday. You on your final warning too?

Imogene   I wish. I'd love to be expelled. I hate this place.

Eamonn   So what were you in there for then? Private audience with the principal? Spill.

Imogene   Only if you tell me what happened to your hand.

Eamonn   I was feedin the birds behind the Home Ec room, giving them their daily bread, as you do, and a jealous seagull swooped down and pecked my hand to bits. Fucking seagulls these days eh? They're mentalists. Your turn. What were you in with Fitzy for?

Imogene   Just some shit about people saying I'm too thin.

Eamonn   Go on.

Imogene   Apparently pupils and teachers are *concerned* about me. It's fucking ridiculous.

Eamonn *laughs.*

Eamonn   You know I've been in that office for every possible offence under the sun. But I've never got a bollocking for being too skinny . . . fair play t'ya.

Caol   We're not too skinny our goals are yet to be achieved // if you think we're thin then you're deceived // we've miles to go stones and pounds // we're still too thick, too chunky, too round.

Eamonn   I hate Fitzy almost as much as he hates me. He's a nasty piece of work. But on this one, I can kinda see where he is coming from.

Imogene   It's none of his business. Or anyone's. It's my life. I don't know why everyone suddenly thinks they're entitled to interfere.

Eamonn   Why d'ya do it then? The not eating thing? If you don't mind me askin? Is it your way of rebelling? Is it two fingers to your mother? Or society? Or what?

Imogene   I don't want to talk about it.

Eamonn   I'm not gonna fuckin judge ye right? I know what they say about you. That you're skinny just to be superior. Willing to die just to look like something off 'America's Next Top Model'. They're narrow-minded fucks.

Imogene   Believe me I've heard it all. Rhino Murphy claims he'd rather shag the fattest woman on earth than go near me with a barge pole. And Melissa and Amy have a bet on about when I'm gonna die.

Eamonn   Shower a cunts. (*Silence.*) But why d'ya do it though? Like when I fuck shit up it's not just for a bit of light entertainment, it's cos I'm fucked off. At teachers mostly. Constantly asking about my home life, properly prying like 'Is everything all right at home Eamonn?' 'Is there something going on at home we should know about?' They want you to cry on their shoulders, confess your ma's an alcoholic, your da's in prison. They fuckin know that shit already. It's all over my file and god knows they spend enough time readin it, and adding to it, and analysin it. And I know they don't want to hate me. They want to make excuses for me, and pity me, and blame my shitty background. But I don't need their sympathy. I just want them to treat me like a person and not an animal that should be in fuckin care. I was just wondering if it's the same for you?

Imogene   Well my dad's not in prison. He could be actually for all I know. If being a massive dick was a crime he definitely would be. But then I suppose the prison system would collapse.

Silence.

Imogene   You mean is it cos I'm angry? The not eating thing . . .?

Eamonn   Ya . . . like you're not just doing cos you want to look like one of them H&M bikini models I presume?

Imogene   No. It's not about . . . it's . . . I don't know. It's a control thing. It's just something I have to do. At first it was just a routine, and now it's more like an addiction. Exercising, losing weight is a high. And gaining it, well it's not really an option. And it's not an attention thing like everyone thinks, it's the opposite. All I want is people to give me space. And I know people think it's extreme but for now this is what I need to do. I don't have a choice.

Eamonn   Heavy.

Imogene   Sorry.

Eamonn   Heavy as your Ma's period. You'll be OK though. You're tough.

Imogene   Is it true you take pills during school hours?

Eamonn   Nah man that's a vicious myth. I'm a natural buzzer. Walking around with this head on my shoulders is like being permanently yipped. Weed is all I do myself.

Imogene   Any chance of a joint now?

Eamonn   You willing to pay for it?

Imogene   Not a chance.

Eamonn   Ah Imo, you're a hard one to refuse.

Scene Eleven

Imogene, **Fionnuala** *and* **Tara** *are in the kitchen.* **Fionnuala** *and* **Tara** *have already eaten.* **Imogene** *is sipping water.* **Caol** *is lurking behind* **Imogene**.

Fionnuala   Would you like some cucumber in your water pet?

Tara   Eamonn Delaney put a hurley through our classroom window today.

Imogene   What?

Fionnuala   Would you like some cucumber with your water?

Tara   They don't call him Demented Delaney for nothing. He's a fucking basket case. Mrs Casey asked him some really generic question, like was everything all right at home, and he completely lost his shit.

Fionnuala   Or a few carrot sticks? I bought some lovely organic vegetables today. I could boil you some?

Imogene   Really?

Fionnuala   Of course love! There's heaps of them in the fridge. I'll put them on for you now.

Tara   Apparently his mum's alcoholic. Like a real one. Like even worse than you Mum.

Fionnuala (*chopping vegetables frantically*)   There's grapes in the fruit bowl too. The red seedless ones you like. Washed and ready to eat.

Tara   He smashed two entire panes of glass and legged it out of the classroom.

Imogene   Maybe he was just having an off day . . .

Tara   An off day? He nearly drowned Ryan McGrath in the disabled bathroom last week because he slagged off his mother.

Imogene   Don't you think he's kind of hilarious?

Tara   What's hilarious about shoving someone's head down the toilet?

Imogene   OK, well that's obviously a bit problematic. I just mean in general he's just a joker, a rebel. And people like that are sometimes misunderstood.

Tara   He's not misunderstood. He's a fucking terrorist. I can't wait till he is gone from our class.

Imogene   What do you mean gone?

Tara   They're expelling him.

Imogene   What? That's fucked!

Tara   No it's not, it's justice.

Imogene   They can't just kick him out.

Tara   Course they can. He's had thousands of warnings. And Mrs Casey is pressing charges for the cuts on her hand from the broken glass.

Caol   The greatest news I've heard all day // he'd be more than expelled if I had my way // your crazy boyfriend is in the bad books // he fooled you wooed you had you hooked // Now forget him drop it focus on us // look at me, am I not enough?

Fionnuala   I'll have these ready for you in ten minutes. They'll be delicious. I won't put any butter or oil on them, right? You can watch me cook them. I swear on my life I won't add a thing.

Tara   Why do you care about Demented Delaney anyway?

Caol   Tell her confess your pathetic crush // fallen for the psycho, fallen in love // desperate to be liked, fancied, desired // had enough of me fed up too tired // to focus on the sacred goals we set // get back upstairs I demand respect.

Tara   Imo, your vegetables.

Imogene   Mum, I'm sorry, I'm . . . I don't want them.

Tara   For christ sake you need to eat something.

Imogene *and* **Caol**   No.

Caol   What part of no don't you understand // no matter how hard you try we refuse to expand.

Fionnuala   Imogene please I'm so tired. I'm so tired of this.

Fionnuala *slides down the cooker and begins to cry.*

Caol   We're going upstairs to skip to the beat // please excuse us while we retreat // no more teenage romance gaining us pounds // back to the drawing board the familiar sound // of skipping burning disappearing // no more meddling scumbag interfering.

Fionnuala   I can't do this anymore. I can't . . . I can't.

Imogene *and* **Caol** *exit.* **Fionnuala** *bursts into tears and* **Tara** *rushes over to comfort her.*

Scene Twelve

Eamonn *and* **Imogene** *are drinking vodka from a bottle, down by the canal. It's getting dark.* **Caol** *is sulking at a distance.* **Eamonn** *plays Maniac 2000 on his iPhone and they both dance madly.*

Imogene   This stuff is rank.

Eamonn   It's my ma's favourite. It's all we ever have in the house. Sometimes when there's no milk I have it on my Rice Crispies.

Imogene (*smiles and hiccups*)   So what are you gonna do? Next.

Eamonn   Finish this bottle and then move on to the next. This stuff is grim, but if I don't drink it my ma will. So it's either this or fuck it down the sink.

Imogene   I mean what's your plan, after you leave here.

Eamonn   Deal I suppose.

Imogene   Deal as in deal with life? Or deal as in deal drugs.

Eamonn   The latter.

Imogene   Is that really what you want to do?

Eamonn   You mean is it my long-term life ambition to sell weed to fund my mother's alcohol addiction. Not really.

Imogene   Why don't you go somewhere else, get out of here?

Eamonn   I can't just up and leave my ma.

Imogene   I thought you hated her.

Eamonn   Of course I don't hate my ma. Her drinkin drives me insane. But I can't blame her. She's had a fucked-up life and all I've done is make it worse. She blames herself for everything I've done. Might be better for her if I left, but I can't bring myself to. Every other man in her life has walked out on her. It just feels wrong.

Imogene   Your dad left. Mine too. Just cos men are dicks to their wives doesn't mean that you can't do something with your life.

Eamonn   What are *you* gonna do with yours so?

Imogene   Get away from here. And then figure things out. I can't think straight these days. I need to be on my own somewhere. Like move to the sea or the top of a mountain.

Eamonn   And you think you'd be OK in the wilderness? On your own.

Imogene   I'd be fine. I like being alone.

Eamonn   You'd disappear.

Imogene   Just for a while.

Eamonn   No I mean you'd physically disappear. You'd waste away. You're not well enough to live on your own. You'd be like the lad in *Into the Wild*.

Imogene   You sound like my mother, and my sister and every other person I thought you were sounder than. It's my fucking life, if I want to live alone and live off a few wild berries and a single bowl of vegetable soup a day then that's what I'll do.

Eamonn   That's the dream then is it? You and your illness holed up in the middle of nowhere sipping Weight Watcher soup and admiring the view till you collapse?

Imogene   Maybe. Why do you care anyway?

Eamonn   Well you're here asking me what I want to do with life, making me feel guilty for going nowhere fast and yet you're telling me your greatest ambition is to starve yourself?

Imogene   I like hanging out with you because you don't try and fix me. Please don't start now.

Eamonn   It would be a waste of my energy anyway wouldn't it? You even want to get better do you?

Imogene   Maybe I don't.

Silence.

Eamonn   It's been good. Getting to know you.

Imogene   Yeah . . . you'll be around though. You just said you weren't leaving.

Eamonn   I can't see you any more Imo. My ma's dying. Her liver's fucked and I can't watch another person self-destruct. I can't do it.

Imogene   But this, whatever this is, it's not . . . it's . . . it's just cigarettes. Behind a shitty prefab. And I'm sorry about your mam but I don't see how that's a reason for us not to be friends. Eamonn, please . . .

Eamonn *kisses her.*

Eamonn   Good luck Imo. Look after yourself. Or don't. Whatever.

Scene Thirteen

Imogene *is lying on the floor in her room staring at the ceiling.* **Caol** *is draped across her.* **Fionnuala** *taps gently on the door.* **Imogene** *ignores her. Eventually* **Fionnuala** *lets herself in.*

Fionnuala   Imogene.

Imogene   Mother.

Fionnuala   May I sit?

Fionnuala *sits on the bed.*

Fionnuala   Imogene, pet, you know I love you. You know that don't you? Oh gosh. Look at us. How did it come to this? You know people warn you that parenting will be tough, but I never imagined it would be like this. And it's so much harder on your own. I hope one day you'll understand.

Imogene   What do you want?

Fionnuala   To talk to you pet. About your eating. It's all gotten a bit out of hand and I'm really worried about you.

Caol   Finally the wagon has opened her eyes // smelt the coffee and recognised // our self-destruction slow demise // but she can't stop us now we've our eye on the prize.

Imogene   Mum I don't have the energy for this.

Fionnuala   We'll exactly that's the point isn't it. You don't have an ounce of energy in you, and yet you're up here exercising round the clock and only consuming a handful of calories a day.

Imogene   I'm keeping fit.

Caol   Desperately jealous of her thin and bone // can't bear this anna girl in her home // under her roof restricting with ease // no surprises that poor old Mum's displeased // she can only dream of such willpower // the interfering green-eyed coward.

Fionnuala　Imogene, I just want to chat. I'm so tired of fighting with you. I want us to be friends again.

Imogene　We were never friends Mum, now can you please leave my room.

Fionnuala　Imogene, do not speak to me in that tone. I am your mother.

Imogene　Congratulations, you shoved me out your vagina. I'm sure you'll get your reward in heaven.

Fionnuala　I'm your mother and I'm worried about you. I'm worried sick. Can't you see what you're putting us through? I can't sleep at night. If I'm not lying awake listening to you pounding around up here, I'm fretting over you destroying your metabolism, annihilating your thyroid gland, weakening your bones. And the more internet research I do the more panicked I get. Malnutrition in the teenage years is directly linked to infertility.

Caol　So she's an expert now, with powers of diagnosis // if only other people could keep their noses // out of our business, stop pretending they care // interfering mother would never dare // admit that she wishes she could disappear too // the dieting mum that's nothing new // look in the mirror where does insecurity stem // from her of course the clucking mother hen.

Imogene　So you don't actually care about me. You care about your beauty sleep, and your future grandchildren?

Tara *enters.*

Fionnuala　No Imogene, I care about *you*. Do you hear me? I care about you more than you will ever understand. Until you have your own children you can't possibly grasp the depth of that love and the pain you experience when your child is suffering.

Imogene   Well I'm on the fast track to infertility, so I guess I'll always be in the dark about this incredible unconditional love.

Fionnuala   That's exactly my point Imogene, you're throwing your future away. You're breaking my heart here. And not only mine but your sister's as well. Can't you see how selfish you're being?

Imogene   Get out of my room Mum. Get out of my room and go back to googling whatever fictitious disease you think I have.

Fionnuala   There is nothing fictitious about this! You're starving yourself Imogene, and you won't even talk to me! It's this attitude, this refusal to communicate that left me with no choice but to contact your father.

Imogene   Wait, what? What has *he* got to do with this?!

Tara   He knows Imo, Mum told him everything.

Imogene   What is wrong with you both? How dare you contact him?! Mum you swore . . . you swore you wouldn't speak to him.

Fionnuala   He may not be our favourite person Imogene, but he is your father and right now I can't seem to manage on my own.

Imogene   You've never been able to manage on your own. Why involve him now? He abandoned us. He left you, he left us, for a woman half your age! Have you no dignity?

Fionnuala   I have spoken to your father and we've decided together, that you need a break. From school, from home, from the skipping, not to mention the skipping of meals. Your father has arranged a place for you in hospital.

Imogene   What?

Fionnuala   Not a hospital, that's the wrong word. A clinic. A residential clinic. And it has an excellent reputation. It's all sorted. This is going to be good for you Imogene.

Imogene   I don't . . . I'm not going

Fionnuala   This isn't open for discussion Imogene. It's all arranged, and paid for I'll be dropping you off tomorrow morning. You'll be there for a couple of months. So get packing.

Imogene *and* **Caol**   Go fuck yourself.

Fionnuala   I'm sorry Imogene I just can't let you live like this under my roof. It's for your sister's sake too . . .

Imogene   Oh so this is a communal decision now is it?

Tara   She has to do something. We can't just stand here while disappear in front of our eyes. I feel like an accessory to you starving yourself. And you won't even talk to us. The only person you speak to is demented Delaney. How do you think that makes me feel?!

Imogene   His name is Eamonn, and he is not demented.

Tara   He's a bully!

Imogene   You have never even spoken to him in your life.

Tara   I feel like I don't know you any more Imo. And I'm trying – we're trying to understand. We are *trying* to help you! I don't know what's happening to you Imo . . . this thing, this condition, it's a monster

Caol   Monster she says, the stupid slob // the ignorant wench attempting to rob // you of your personal freedom your right to live // the way you choose, she could possibly give // less of a shit about your welfare // be brave my child do not despair // united and fading we'll disappear // we have each other don't you fear.

Imogene   I do *not* need help.

Caol   Look at me Imo your mine I'm yours // we're winning they can't bear to see us lose // more and more weigh it's a sign of success // don't let the sway you, it's a trap it's a test // of how much you trust me how loyal you'll be // don't betray, don't make me angry.

Tara   Imo, *please*. It's not forever. If we don't do something this thing is gonna kill you. Imo look at me. Why won't you look at me?!

Caol   Run! Run for the hills and never look back // if we flee now we'll survive intact // it's make or break its fight or flight // we'll never be separated the ends in sight.

Imogene *and* **Caol** *run out of the house.* **Tara** *follows, desperate to catch* **Imogene** *before she runs herself into the ground.*

Tara   Imo wait! Please! **Imogene**!

Tara *steps out onto the road and is hit by a car.*

Scene Fourteen

Tara *is unconscious in a hospital bed.* **Fionnuala** *is sitting beside her, holding her hand.* **Imogene** *enters, with a cup of tea for* **Fionnuala**. **Caol** *is absent.*

Imogene   How is she?

Fionnuala   OK. The same. I thought I saw her eyes flicker but I think I imagined it.

You look exhausted.

Imogene   I'm all right. Are you OK?

Fionnuala   I'm fine pet. Don't worry about me. I got her favourite pyjamas from home. I hate seeing her in that horrible hospital gown. She'd much prefer to be in her pink silks.

Imogene   I don't think she minds too much right now. I'm sorry Mum.

Fionnuala   Don't be sorry love. It's not your fault.

Tara *wakes up. She is weak and disorientated.*

Tara   Imo . . .

Imogene   She's awake. Tara, you're awake!

Fionnuala   Thank god, oh sweet Jesus thank god you're OK.

Tara   Imo, where am I?

Imogene   Sssssh Tara, you're OK. You're in hospital, but you're fine. Everything's gonna be fine.

Tara   I'll have a sex on the beach.

Fionnuala   What? What did you say Tara pet?

Tara   I'm so thirsty, I'll have a sex on the beach.

Imogene   She wants a cocktail.

Fionnuala   You're all confused love, you're in hospital you can't have a cocktail.

Imogene   You had an accident Tara. But you're gonna be fine. You'll be out in no time and the first thing we'll do is go out for cocktails.

Tara   I'll have a sex on the beach.

Fionnuala   You will not! You'll have a good clean orange juice!

Imogene   Don't worry Tara, we'll get sloshed, all three of us, on the most expensive, delicious sex on the beaches you've ever tasted.

Tara   Who's here?

Imogene   It's just us. Just mum and me.

Imogene's Letter to Eamonn IV

Caol *is no where to be seen.*

Imogene   They're moving Tara from ICU soon. Her pelvis is broken as are six of her ribs but they say the head injury is less serious than they initially thought so we are so relieved. I can't even bear to think about how close we came to losing her.

Caol *emerges from the shadows and begins to drag herself slowly and painfully towards* **Imogene**.

The last time I saw you, you said I'd never get better, because I didn't want to. And I'm writing to tell you I am going to prove you wrong. I want to catch a glimpse of myself in a shop window and not feel disgust. I want to go on holiday with Mum and Tara and not pack my skipping rope. I want to look in the mirror and see a precious functioning body that can breathe and move, and love, and run for a bus without collapsing.

And I'm so scared Eamonn. I'm so scared that now I've decided I want to change, I won't be able to. And I know this sounds awful but I'm afraid that without out it I'll be nothing. I can barely remember the person I was before. I feel like this . . . madness has crept in and stolen a vital part of Imogene.

Mostly though, I'm just scared of life without you. It's so strange not seeing you. I think about you all the time. I hope that in the future I can see you again. We'll meet down by the canal, and you'll dazzle me with your smile. And you'll be OK, and I'll be OK too.

Imo.

Caol, *who is now at* **Imogen**'s *feet, bangs loudly on the ground.*

The End.

 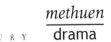

Bloomsbury Methuen Drama Modern Plays

include work by

Bola Agbaje
Edward Albee
Davey Anderson
Jean Anouilh
John Arden
Peter Barnes
Sebastian Barry
Alistair Beaton
Brendan Behan
Edward Bond
William Boyd
Bertolt Brecht
Howard Brenton
Amelia Bullmore
Anthony Burgess
Leo Butler
Jim Cartwright
Lolita Chakrabarti
Caryl Churchill
Lucinda Coxon
Curious Directive
Nick Darke
Shelagh Delaney
Ishy Din
Claire Dowie
David Edgar
David Eldridge
Dario Fo
Michael Frayn
John Godber
Paul Godfrey
James Graham
David Greig
John Guare
Mark Haddon
Peter Handke
David Harrower
Jonathan Harvey
Iain Heggie

Robert Holman
Caroline Horton
Terry Johnson
Sarah Kane
Barrie Keeffe
Doug Lucie
Anders Lustgarten
David Mamet
Patrick Marber
Martin McDonagh
Arthur Miller
D. C. Moore
Tom Murphy
Phyllis Nagy
Anthony Neilson
Peter Nichols
Joe Orton
Joe Penhall
Luigi Pirandello
Stephen Poliakoff
Lucy Prebble
Peter Quilter
Mark Ravenhill
Philip Ridley
Willy Russell
Jean-Paul Sartre
Sam Shepard
Martin Sherman
Wole Soyinka
Simon Stephens
Peter Straughan
Kate Tempest
Theatre Workshop
Judy Upton
Timberlake Wertenbaker
Roy Williams
Snoo Wilson
Frances Ya-Chu Cowhig
Benjamin Zephaniah

For a complete catalogue
of Bloomsbury Methuen Drama
titles write to:

Bloomsbury Methuen Drama
Bloomsbury Publishing Plc
50 Bedford Square
London WC1B 3DP

or you can visit our website at:
www.bloomsbury.com/drama

9 781474 291088